HOLLAND

Cologne ●

● Bonn

Liége ●

BELGIUM

Frankfurt ●

LUXEM-
BOURG

● Luxembourg

GERMANY

DUGOUT OF THE
CROWN PRINCE

✳

✳   ✳
LE CLAON   VERDUN

MEUSE ●
St. Mihiel

1914 BORDER

● Nancy

Strasbourg ●

River Marne

FRANCE

VOSGES

OLD
ARMAND
✳

Freiburg ●

MONTREUX-JEUNE
(LE MOULIN DE LA CAILLE)
Belfort ●

✳

JONCHEREY ✳

Basel ●

● Dijon

SWITZERLAND

Still Quiet on the Western Front

Fifty Years Later

GENE SMITH

Still Quiet on the Western Front
Fifty Years Later

DRAWINGS BY BILL BERRY
INTRODUCTION BY S. L. A. MARSHALL

WILLIAM MORROW & CO.   NEW YORK 1965

By the Same Author

THE LIFE AND DEATH OF SERGE RUBINSTEIN

WHEN THE CHEERING STOPPED: *The Last Years
of Woodrow Wilson*

Contents

JONCHEREY: "TWO BOYS"   1

LE MOULIN DE LA CAILLE:

    "THE GREAT FIGHT"   18

O VERDUN!   25

THE DUGOUT OF THE CROWN PRINCE:

    "I WOULD KNOW IT"   39

LA VILLE-AUX-BOIS-LES-PONTAVERT:

    NINE HUNDRED AND SEVENTY-THREE   53

BELLEAU WOOD: "WE ARE PROUD

    TO BEAR THE TITLE"   61

THE SOMME: DOOLIS HAY   69

YPRES: KENNEY   81

YPRES: THE MENIN GATE   102

Photographs

The photographs which are used in this book originally appeared in an exhibition at the Imperial War Museum, London, which opened in the autumn of 1964 to commemorate the fiftieth anniversary of the First World War.

The World War I pictures are reproduced here by the kind permission of the Imperial War Museum. The photographs taken in 1964 which show the same locations are printed with the kind permission of Peter G. Masefield. None of these photographs may be reproduced without the written consent of the Museum.

PERVYSE, BELGIUM   10-11

FURNES, BELGIUM   12-13

LONDON, ENGLAND   14-15

LOOS RIDGE, FRANCE   46-47

MONS, BELGIUM   48-49

AMIENS, FRANCE   50-51

ZILLEBEKE ROAD, NEARS YPRES, BELGIUM   92-93

FURNES, BELGIUM   94-95

THE MENIN ROAD, BELGIUM   96-97

YPRES, BELGIUM   98-99

Introduction

For this book, there is already a place in my library alongside a thin volume of essays, "The Wet Flanders Plain," written by the Englishman, Henry Williamson in 1927.

I have prized it these years for the same reasons that hereafter "Still Quiet" will be treasured. The themes are identical. A sensitive man goes as a pilgrim to the old Western Front and finds sermons in rusting shards. Filled with an uncommon anguish, he writes less of what he sees than what he feels. A vast melancholy of spirit and a reverence for life pervade both writings. These emotions I share vicariously with Gene Smith while I read him, grateful that I am thus transported.

Mr. Smith asks the penetrating question: "Was it all in never-never land, far from the American of today?" These are his words as he ponders Belleau Wood, and I rejoice that there was room for this one American field among his reveries. It deserves the perfect tribute, and he has given nothing less. To answer him, however, yes, it is never-never land, as fresh and as unreal as last night's dream. One thing stays vivid, tangible as ever: the recollection of a comradeship that made any misery tolerable.

So his reflections serve me as a takeoff point to some soldier talk about that first A.E.F., the grandest company I ever shared. The mood is heightened as I write this by the approach of Armistice Day. Yes, I know that some years ago President Eisenhower renamed it Veterans Day. But no doughboy who fought on the Western Front and thrilled to its supreme moment when the quiet thickened at the eleventh hour on the eleventh day approves of that or accepts it. Armistice Day it must remain in the name of old buddies and old memories.

Our outfit hit France green as grass and served by a General Staff and logistical backup not much better. We were sent to train at a village named Bure-les-

Templieres not more than two miles from where the source of the Seine bubbles up from under a limerock cliff.

Rumor told us the village name meant "burial ground of the Templars." True or false, no soldier had ever set foot on that ground since the Templars were planted. Every cobbled street was over-incrusted with a five-inch paving of hardened manure. The Roman roads had not been longer lost to France under a millennium of debris. But it was wonderfully springy to walk upon, something halfway between a crepe sole and a trampoline.

We would have kept it that way for posterity, there being too little bounce in this life. Down came that hard foot of our over-sensitive higher authority. Before we were permitted to drill, goldbrick or fire a Chauchat (that evil French light machine gun was ironically nick-named "sure shot"), we had to get out with picks and shovels and divest our billet area of the overlay. It was like trying to spade a sea of vitrified rubber. But by the end of one week, we had it made, all in the name of U.S. Army sanitary standards. Bure-les-Templieres began to shine and smell like a gardenia, though the cows kept coming, and for our labor of destruction, the villagers from cowherd to mayor loathed us.

By that time we were discovering that the bounty of our own grateful Republic and the efficiency of its supply services were somewhat less than the guidebooks say. Early we ran out of tobacco, which along with cooking whiskey and chocolate were as unprocurable as ambergris. Moreover, week followed week and not a chew or cough-in-a-carload came our way.

Came the great day when at last one small consignment of tobacco dropped amid us like manna. It was Bull Durham only—the makin's—and not in quantity sufficient to go more than one-fourth the way around. Followed a council of war among junior leaders and of it came the Great Decision. The Durham would be given the chewers and the smokers would continue to wait. It was a judgment worthy of Solomon or Stonewall. The smokers cheered it out of compassion for the boys who had nicotine hunger in their bones. They were rewarded by the spectacle of the chewers wolfing down those dry flakes the way a hungry logger goes at beans.

That was an expeditionary force which had a lovely time talking about the wonderful, commonplace things you might some day enjoy provided you lasted; things like potatoes, carrots, dad-ratted-green-gutted turnips, a pair sunny-side up, coffee with cream, sauerkraut and delectable fresh meat, such as round steak, hamburger and hot dogs. One of my fellow sergeants, who was bothered by a sweet tooth, always polished off the evening meal by talking about cheese cake.

In those early weeks we got no green vegetables or variety from the tins. Only two items came through in large bulk to fortify the training menu. The messkits were laden with canned salmon until they turned pink. We had not known there were 341 ways to prepare salmon or that it was considered a breakfast dish. The other *pièce de résistance* was fresh onions. The U.S. seemed to be in a conspiracy to bury our regiment under this one vegetable.

Candy? In two years overseas, I saw one small chocolate bar, and for that I paid eighty francs at a time when five francs would buy a bottle of champagne. There was no Coca-Cola ration and such brew as we had were the beers of Meuse and Moselle, tasting like the undiluted waters of those streams. Our best eating was Welch's Grapelade and canned browned beef hash. The usual fare in combat was black coffee, French hard biscuits and a slab of bully beef. Well I remember that on the Thanksgiving following the Armistice the only unusual item on the menu was some brown sugar that the cook had baked to a crisp.

Another difference between that Old Show and the

later ones was that outside of one's rations and ammo, almost nothing expendable came free. What you got you paid for, which was fair enough, but for the moratorium on pay. Summer would pass, and the first frosts arrive, still without a paycall.

As for leave time, during training in the United States, if your mother died or your home burned down, or you broke a leg and were no good to the service anyway, you might get a ten-day furlough. Otherwise, nix, no matter come Thanksgiving, Christmas or the end of a training phase. Overseas, when the show was on, you stayed at your post. The only respite from duty was in those precious days when the outfit rested between fronts. Then you could watch the French trample the grapes with their bare feet and still drink their wine with a relish, while eating the village white bread like a gift from the gods, because it seemed so very, very good to be alive and out of danger.

Yes, there was entertainment. But no Hopes, Bennys and Dietrichs barnstormed the front to amuse troops and make work easy for their own press agents. There was only Elsie Janis. When the war was over, the A.E.F. organized its own vaudeville circuit out of soldier talent. While it was on, the only music heard by troops were the songs we sang as we slogged the dusty road—"Pack Up Your Troubles," "Long, Long Trail," "Lulu" and "Frankie and Johnny." When there was no other way to relieve boredom up front we played little kids' games such as duck-on-the-rock, hop-scotch and drop-the-handkerchief—"hot ass," we called it. Catch, volley ball and horseshoes would have been better, but when that Army was committed to fighting it was stripped of all such equipment.

Our uniforms were about as unsightly as anything the mind of man might devise. Our rifles were poorly made and inaccurately sighted. Our other weapons were almost non-existent, and had it not been for help from our Allies, we could not have fought. We many times had to bury our own dead during battle. We were never carried to any point that was within maximum walking range. Not knowing any better, our superiors kept as much weight on our backs as possible, hoping to build muscle, instead of lightening the burden to refresh the spirit.

Despite all of that, there was respect in us for higher authority and full belief in the sanctity of an order. We had faith in our people, love for our country and happiness in our hearts. We were not blind to our difficulties. We were not unaware that some of the load might have been lightened for us by greater thoughtfulness in others. We simply saw these things as incidental, as part of the normal inheritance of man in a far-from-perfect universe. Above and beyond every small consideration was the understanding that our land was in danger, that we had been called on, that we had to do what we could.

Such was the attitude of Pershing's A.E.F. It was a crude Army by present standards, unreasonably self-confident, high-humored, boisterous, cocky, almost vulgarly so. But Man, how we loved it, and Man, how we strove to help one another! Nothing felt since has made the heart leap so.

So this late in the game I dare speak up for the "fat and bald old men" of Gene Smith's moving story. When we hear the cynics say that our all-outness marked us as a particularly naïve generation, we smile. The cynics were not there; they do not know. We think of ourselves as the lucky survivors of the Grand Fellowship. It gave us the best days of our lives and a firmer hold on the future than those less fortunate than we.

S.L.A. Marshall

Dherran Dhoun,
Birmingham, Michigan

S.L.A. Marshall, Brigadier General USAR-Ret., served from private in the Engineer Corps to first lieutenant in the Infantry with the American Expeditionary Forces in France during the First World War. He is the author of many books, most recently *The American Heritage History of World War I*.

Joncherey: *"Two Boys"*

I⊤ IS IN the late afternoons that the road to Faverois comes alive. The cows are ambling back from the fields, driven on their way by old women and little boys. The few automobiles and tractors crawl along behind the slow cattle, and chickens scrabbling in the mud run clucking away. When the cows are in their barns, the road falls silent. After nine o'clock it is completely empty and not one car an hour will go by.

The First World War began on this road. There is a monument on the exact spot. It celebrates Jules André Peugeot, corporal of the 44th Regiment of Infantry. On August 2, 1914, some thirty hours before the declaration of war between Germany and France, Peugeot and four soldiers with him gave letters home to the local mail carrier, who took them and went off. There was a house then where now there is the monument. The daughter of the house went across this road to the spring from which the family and the soldiers got their water. At the edge of a field she saw horsemen. They wore spiked helmets. The girl ran, screaming, "The Prussians!" Corporal Peugeot came out of the house carrying a rifle. He stood on the slight rise where his monument is now and saw, coming toward him at a gallop, a German officer on a horse. He raised his rifle and shouted, "Stop there!" The German, who was Lieutenant Camille Mayer, had a revolver in his hand. On it was written in Latin, "For the War." He fired it three times past his horse's head. Peugeot fired back.

Mayer swayed in the saddle. His horse passed the house and kept going. Peugeot turned and reeled. Four shots.

It had been a very hot summer, and the roads and fields of this wet region would have been drier than usual. So when Peugeot fell across the threshold of the house, and Mayer slid out of his saddle, each would have found dust rather than mud. The site of their encounter was never to be important again, for there

was little subsequent fighting there. The nearest big battlefield is a few miles north, on a high peak whose actual name is the Hartsmannwillerkopf, but which the French soldiery of fifty years ago termed "Old Armand." It is part of the eastern face of the Vosges Mountains, which look down across the flat plains of Alsace leading the few miles to Switzerland.

On Old Armand the trench lines wind off in all directions, resembling choked medieval moats. Moss grows from the top of dugouts and there are great piles of rusting barbed wire. It is difficult to walk over the area; the barbed wire hidden in the undergrowth tears at the shoes and one falls into shell holes. Parents warn their children to be careful of the rusted sheet metal dangling from the dugout ceilings, and scold them when they scrape themselves on the barbed-wire spurs, which, perhaps dulled by the long years, are no longer really very sharp. Through the holes cut in the thick steel of the machine-gun emplacements—the little doors to cover the holes still swing gratingly shut—the children bend and squint to see Switzerland's mountains in the haze. There is a cemetery and a crypt on Old Armand. In front of each grave, with its insignia MORT POUR LA FRANCE, a rose bush is growing, and before some, relatives have long ago placed little

ENGLAND

● Ostend

FLANDERS

● Calais

✳ YPRES
● **MENIN**

Brussels ●

A
R
T
O
I
S

P
I
C
A
R
D
Y

River Somme

Arras ●

● Cambrai

✳ **ALBERT**

AMIENS ✳

AISNE

● Laon

LA VILLE-
AUX-BOIS-
LES-
PONTAVERT

● Rouen

**LE CHEMIN
DES DAMES**

Compiègne ●

✳

● Soissons

River Seine

BELLEAU WOOD ✳

Château-Thierry ●

● Reims

✳

River Seine

C
H
A
M
P
A
G
N
E

Paris ●

River Seine

**KEY
THE WESTERN FRONT**
September, 1917 — — —
June 26, 1918 ● ● ● ● ● ● ●
August 15, 1918 ━━━━━

memorials: A crucified Jesus Christ, a few stone flowers. In front of one of the graves there is a small plaque perhaps eight inches square. On one half of it, protected by glass, there is a picture of a young man with a military mustache. Under the picture is written: *To the memory of Jules Pierre, Sergeant of the 152nd Regiment of Infantry. Fallen on the 26th of March, 1916*. On the other half of the plaque is a picture of a round-faced and serious little boy. Under the child's picture is: *To our little Jules. Darling*.

People pose their children in front of the high flagpole with the tricolor waving in the wind over the graves of those who, had it all been different, would have been grandfathers to children like these. In this high stony place there is a notice that visitors are in the presence of tens of thousands of soldiers who fought for France, and down in the crypt are flowers given by The Blinded of France and The Colonies in Honor of Their Valiant Comrades, and a simple cross, really just two pieces of wood, placed by the Boy Scouts of France and Germany before a pedestal topped with a corroding helmet. There is a Jewish star upon one stone wall and under it: "From the four winds come O Spirit and blow upon these. . . ." and, on another wall, the words: "I am the Resurrection." In

the middle, waist-high, is a drum-shaped bronze memorial as large as a living room. Upon its top is: *La
Patrie.*

In Joncherey there is but the little monument. Only a
slight exercise of imagination is needed, however, to
project one's mind back to the summer of 1914, that
beautiful time ever after remembered as the sweetest
months of men's lives, to where Corporal Peugeot is
lying dead across the threshold of the house and Lieutenant Mayer is dead upon the road. After Mayer's
patrol scatters into the woods, the two dead soldiers
are picked up and put on a bed of straw in the local
grange. They lie side by side for several hours. Then
they are buried. Peugeot in civilian life was a schoolteacher. His mother was a schoolteacher, too. He was
twenty-one years old. Mayer, the official French report
said, was twenty to twenty-two years old "at the most."
His horse was taken by the French military authorities
and given a new name: "Joncherey."

For them, the first of the millions, the Schlieffen
Plan would crash in the north and *àl'outrance, à la
baionette* would rush forward in the south. Children
would starve in the hills of Budapest, and the Crown
Prince of Germany would write the King of England
from his place of exile to complain that he did not even

[9]

Imperial War Museum

PERVYSE, BELGIUM. The bodies of French soldiers lie heaped before a church whose roof has been destroyed and whose walls seared by the fire of the Third and Twenty-Second Reserve Corps of the advancing German Army. November, 1914.

PERVYSE, BELGIUM. The roof has been replaced; the walls redone. The glass is back in the windows. And the French soldiers are buried in the church yard on the right. Springtime of 1964.

FURNES, BELGIUM. Machine gun cars of the British Navy attached to the Royal Naval Air Service in the town square.

Peter G. Masefield

FURNES, BELGIUM. The houses are the same, the church
is the same, even the cobblestones are the same. But the machine
gun cars are gone. And most of the Limeys have died young.

have a bathroom in his house. One day, four decades after it was put in place, a giant mine detonated by lightning hitting a willow tree would blast Belgian tiles off the roofs of a hundred houses not far from where Lieutenant-Colonel Winston Churchill and Obergefreiter Adolf Hitler both served. Czar of Russia would raise his arms to stop the bullets coming at his wife and children, and President of the United States would issue a statement that he much regretted the passing of Sergeant Alvin C. York. Marshals of France would go to the shrine of Jeanne D'Arc to offer thanks for victory, and the Prince of Wales would wipe his eyes at Remembrance Sunday ceremonies. Remembering Verdun, Von Falkenhayn would find it hard to sleep for all the rest of his life, and Plumer's hair would turn white during his years of command at Ypres. The million old maids of France— people called them The Waiting Ones—would be a political force of tremendous power, and a woman in Chicago, gone from Europe forty years, would write to the head of the Czech Volunteers Association in Paris to ask if she could name the place of her brother's grave; if so, she would come, old enough to be his grandmother and with the old country's language half-forgotten, to stand where he sleeps forever young.

Today the curé of the town, Father Marcel Holder, does not speak of the Boche and the Frenchman, or even the German and the Frenchman. Only of two boys who killed each other.

Le Moulin de la Caille:
"The Great Fight."

THE WIND always blows here; it was a good place for the windmill they called Le Moulin de la Caille—The Windmill of the Quail. There are no cars on the dingy winding road, no passers-by or motor-bikes. It is said that along the line of the Western Front from Belfort to Ostend there has been an emptiness and silence since 1918, and in this place it does seem so. There is nothing nomadic about the French, and no new people have moved here. And most of the boys who lived here in 1914 are now dead, and their sons and daughters who-might-have-been have never lived. So it is very quiet where the French and the Germans fought the battle of Le Moulin de la Caille.

The storehouse of the mill stands, although the mill has fallen into ruins. The son of the farmer who owned it in August of 1914 when the Germans came can remember very well how it was in his father's day: there were the same trees, and the stream was the same. Perhaps the area under cultivation was larger and less of the countryside was given over to forest. Perhaps it was less lonely. But the fight was like this: the French lived in the mill—there. A worker was cutting hay with a scythe across the stream. He saw the Germans. He came running to the mill, where marked above the door is the date of its construction: 1781. He banged with his scythe on the door—one sees in imagination the grandmothers of these chickens one hundred times removed running to get out of his way—and cried, "The Germans!" And here is the man: a scraggly mustache, sunken cheeks, watery eyes. When he knocked, the French captain came out and quickly had his men turn over the carriages and carts here by the stream so that there would be a barricade. The captain was around thirty-five years old, he was tall enough, his name was Japy. So the French got down by the carriages under this red tile roof which juts out from the

[19]

walls in order to protect the wood piled up for winter, and they began to shoot. The Germans fired back. Look, here are the bullet marks on the wall. It was very hot and about three in the afternoon. They fought for five hours or so, until dusk. The next day the French left Le Moulin de la Caille and went back about a mile and began to cross this canal. They thought the Germans were still back by the mill, but the Germans had followed them. They were wading through the water when the firing began. It was a carnage. The young-boy-who-was has a thin, lined neck, and it works as he talks. And he says the water was red—really red. And Captain Japy was dead. When Lieutenant Bolle came from Belfort the Germans fired at him and he lost his arm. And so it was over. One still finds cartridges in the fields.

Captain Japy's widow lived until a few years ago. All through Poincaré and Clemenceau, through Léon Blum and the Popular Front, through Pétain and the Resistance, through Liberation and Indochina and Algeria, she lived on, coming Sunday after Sunday, birthday after birthday, Armistice Day after Armistice Day, to visit the place where her husband died for France. She never remarried. Lieutenant Bolle recovered from the loss of his arm and became a teacher

and head of the boys' school in Beaucourt, a few miles away. He lived until very recently. His wife remained friendly with Madame Japy, and each Armistice Day they went together with all the other people to hear Professor Bolle, for so he was called, deliver a speech at the little monument by Le Moulin de la Caille. The one-armed professor's war had lasted less than one hour, but for forty-five years he gave a talk each November eleventh. The newspaper of the town always reported that he was eloquent as he described the fight as "glorious" and said that France was proud of her "beautiful soldiers" who fell there. Girls sold, and sell, little decorations made by the Friends of the 235th Regiment of Infantry who, as it says on the monument, "valiantly fought to forbid elements of the 29th and 30th Divisions of Germany access to the soil of France." There was and is fired a salvo of one hundred shots from an artillery piece at dawn. There was a parade, the marchers fewer each year, even though the veterans of the Second War also go to the ceremony in a body. (They have few monuments of their own and never go to the places where they fought in 1940.) Children get up early and collect flowers from the farmers. And the wind blows across the empty fields and parts itself at the little monument with the names of the dead men,

and stirs the shrubs and moves the bouquets placed in
the wire holders attached to the monument when it
was erected, and stings the eyes of those looking at the
raised lettering: "Time removes everything but the
memory"; "But these are in peace." When the day is
finished there is a dinner and the distribution of prizes
from the little lottery which has raised money for the
Friends of the 235th Regiment of Infantry, which
fought and lost 164 soldiers of France at this skirmish,
this one of a million tiny encounters, this unimportant
affair which France and the world have long forgotten
but which in this little area near the town of Montreux-
Jeune is called the big battle, the great fight.

O Verdun!

ALL ALONG the dull road up from Bar-le-Duc there are concrete posts with concrete helmets on top and raised lettering saying that this is La Voie Sacrée, The Sacred Road. At Souilly, Pétain's headquarters building is unchanged from the way it looks in the pictures that show him standing on the steps to watch the youth of a nation go northward to its fate. Seventy per cent of the French Army went up this road. Night and day the trucks went grinding by; battalions of men stood and flung crushed rock under the tires so that they would not sink into the mud. This was the only road the German shells were unable to reach.

Today it is strangely silent, however much one strains to hear the sound of motors and sloshing boots and the mumbled throbbing of the distant places where for months on end the guns were never quiet. But the visible signs of battle are still present. Here are the long trenches, twelve feet deep then, six feet now that nature has half filled them up; here are the craters with cows scrambling up their sides but kept from going into the road by war-time barbed wire strung on screw-pickets fifty years old; here is the metal plate used for protection against the shells and now used to roof sheds and support garden walls. In these fields it is impossible to walk for long without seeing rusted metal protruding up through the wet moss; here if you leave the road and go past the signs warning of mortal danger—Danger of Death!—you will soon lose yourself in the scrub pine planted in the thirties when experts finally decided the soil was too gas- and shell-corrupted to reclaim for agriculture. Under trees or in stream beds are rusted grenades and shells as terrifying as coiled snakes. Dig and you will find bullets, shell fragments, broken rifles, sardine tins, decayed canteens, unidentifiable bits of metal. It requires but a few minutes of work to hold in your hand what was last seen two generations ago by a boy in field gray or horizon blue. Now he is an old man in Leipzig or Nancy or, more likely, he is known as the grandfather or great-uncle who perished at Verdun.

The name on the signposts, seen from a moving car, catches the eye and holds it as the car sweeps past. Verdun. In the city itself, in one of the long deep galleries of the citadel where the French troops found rest during their infrequent respites from the ever-wet trenches (it always rains here), there is a one-eyed veteran. His glass eye never moves. He gives foreigners a piece of paper typed in their language which asks that they not forget to tip him. Inside the gallery one's breath hangs in the air even in August. There are eight coffins covered with oilcloth flags. (No cotton or silk would last long in this dank wet place.) On the wall there is a great sign: THEY SHALL NOT PASS. By the third coffin from the rear a mannequin stands. It wears the uniform of the 132nd Regiment of Infantry, complete with helmet and cartridge cases. The hand holds a bouquet of plastic flowers resting on the coffin. All is as it was when, in November of 1920, a young soldier from the Regiment's honor guard selected for France her Unknown Soldier from among eight Unknowns. When he had placed his flowers on the coffin, it was taken out and with the great and the mighty looking on, carried to Paris, and buried beneath the Arc de Triomphe. The other seven were taken to a cemetery just outside the city, where they lie in a semicircle with the information on a plaque above them that among these could be your father, your son, brother, husband, friend.

Past the seven is the road up to the right bank of the Meuse and the heights where for ten months Crown Prince Wilhelm's army sought the city. The Meuse itself is a dreamy stream where old men equipped with immensely long fishing poles—they must be twenty-five feet in length—troll in the afternoons. The charmless and dull villages up on the heights are composed of but a few score houses each, and the narrow roads are never free of the droppings of the cows. Signs say: "This ground has been the Calvary of soldiers. Every square foot bears the marks of its bloody progress. Complete silence is requested out of respect for the thousands buried here." One comes to a village sign-post which says, Fleury. The town is on all maps. But there is no town. It is gone, along with the other lost towns whose only physical reminders are that now and again, struggling through the thick undergrowth off the roads, someone will turn over a piece of red tile with his foot. Immediately after the war, when all this

was wasteland and the returning refugees smoked constantly to dull the odor of the rotting boys, the government published notices saying that those who had lived here must not return. It took a lot of convincing before those who had lived in Fleury finally gave up and settled down elsewhere. Each year for decades they returned on one day, prayed at the little chapel erected in the woods, and elected a new mayor. They put up a sign where once their main street had been: HERE WAS FLEURY.

Past the terrible sign is a great cemetery. On a hill facing the graves is the Ossuaire. In the rear are a score of windows at waist level. One must bend and shade the eyes to see what is there. Bones are there—the bones of 150,000 unidentified men of both sides. Here is a window: see the neat piles of leg bones. Another: arms. Another: skulls. Another: skulls. Look at the hole in this one. See the spider weaving his web between the eye sockets. Through other windows in the ossuary one sees bones piled in unsorted confusion. This collection is ever-growing; often a wild boar rooting in the earth will show where more bones lie. Or during a forest fire a 75-mm. shell will blow up, fifty years late, and uncover more Unknown Soldiers.

Beyond the ossuary is the Trench of Bayonets. A

shell buried alive a squad of French soldiers here. Only their bayonets protruded above the ground. The soldiers are still there, and their rusting bayonets and rifle muzzles also. Imagination looks down and unearths the lower part of the rifle and the hands and body of him who last touched this weapon. One sees his helmet and decayed rags of blue, perhaps, and metal buckles and the boots. Down there will be ammunition attached to the rotted leather belt, some coins, perhaps a pipe. Above is a concrete roof, erected by an American benefactor, and the visitors. Here is Grandmother, or perhaps it is Great-aunt, coming from the car where she sits behind with the children while the parents have the honored seats in front. By now they are all thoroughly bored with her stories.

A horn blows commandingly from a bus with German license plates; it signals that its passengers must climb aboard so that they may ride to Fort Douaumont. The fort today is a giant formless ruin with a few scarred gun turrets on its top. Near it is the little ravine through which the Germans came in 1916 to capture it and stun a France that believed Douaumont to be the strongest land fortification in the world. (A generation of German schoolboys grew up playing The Capture of Douaumont.) The ravine was called Strawberry Ravine, and the fruit still grows there and is sweet. At the top of the fort one looks out over much of the battlefield; standing on it as nobody safely could for years, one listens for the terrible guns lined up wheel to wheel that made this the most shelled part of the world's surface and left this endless ugly collection of pockmarks. Across these wet fields under these dripping skies the trench lines wind off between the barbed-wire entanglements; in the muddy bottoms of those trenches and over the top strands of that wire France died as a world power. Ever after they haunted France, those dead adolescents and young men of this area little larger than New York's Central Park. (In 1940 the Germans crossed in a quarter of an hour the fields their fathers were never to cross.)

The neatly paved roads—for there are numerous tourists—are the only flat surface in this area. Everywhere else the tortured land rises and dips unevenly. The topsoil has in many places simply vanished, and it is said that any man who lived through Verdun must never have stood still. For every square inch was hit not once but dozens of times. But alone in the deserted scrub pines of Le Mort Homme or in the silent, ever-wet ruins of Poivre it requires the most intense effort to realize that this dead place was the scene of a great

[33]

turning point of history. Joncherey where it all began is different; the name is not famous, nor the event which took place there. One does not expect too much. Joncherey is not in our blood and in our memories; it was not at Joncherey that there perished the legendary officers of the Great War who went into battle carrying their canes and saying to their men, "My dear friends, I will ask you to join me singing 'La Marseillaise' as we go over the top." That was reserved for Verdun, that and the disappearance forever of all represented by France's glorious uniform of red pantaloons, and Germany's wonderfully martial spiked helmets. Madelon and Germania flocked to the stations to kiss the warriors —*"A Berlin!" "Nach Paris!"*—and in the end the trains stopped at Verdun. After terrible Verdun, after the mules drowning in this shell hole here, after the disemboweled boys screaming in this fallen-in dugout, the nineteenth century was over and history was back on the track for what the twentieth was meant to be.

All this happened at Verdun. And yet no drums beat and there are no bugles. You must do it all yourself. Concentrating and looking back past the France and Germany that followed Verdun, past sick France sliding downhill and sick Germany with its monocled politicians in high stiff collars and their leather-booted

prostitutes, you must say to yourself, Here under my feet and within the space I see, hundreds of thousands died, here the world turned over. I am standing where men tipped their helmets forward so the rain would slurp forward; here the artillery fire was as the summits of the hills falling into the deepest valleys; here lazy star shells, beautiful in the dark, their light reflected on the wet rifles—you will find those rifles twelve inches down—floated into the sky and revealed the raiders trapped between the lines. Here the officers on this tiny hill called the roll and ordered the ladders placed and the rations distributed before the charge. "An attack was made yesterday upon the enemy's position. A line of trenches was carried by assault." Nobly wooded for a hundred miles, the heights of the Meuse are covered here with this scrawny pine. This dreary landscape where I stand listening and waiting was the focal point of all the civilizations of the world. Here came the Negroes of France's colonial empire; here came the Bavarians asking, "Are there any Africans opposite?" Here came the young boy friends of the gray and obsequious old maids who make the beds in your Cannes or Paris hotel but who once wrote inspiring letters and knitted mufflers.

There is a guide who lives in the city of Verdun.

His name is Charles Dreyfus. He is vaguely related to the Captain Dreyfus of The Affair. He fought in the war and afterward worked to clear the heights of the live shells, dead animals, human bodies. Now he takes tourists around. For the Americans he explains in his accented English just how it was. With the Germans he is completely correct and precise. The French say, "My grandfather——my uncle——my father——O Verdun!" and there is very little that he has to explain.

The Dugout
of the Crown Prince:

"I Would Know It"

EX-SERGEANT MAJOR POLLE of the 82nd Regiment of
Infantry is looking for the place where he was
wounded. His daughter is with him, and his spinster
sister. (His wife is long dead.) He was back looking in
1961 after an absence of forty-five years, but he
couldn't find the exact place. Now he will try again—
he has driven down from Lille with his daughter for
this reason. There was a quarry near by, he remembers, and a little hill. The trenches of the Germans
were not farther away than the length of an average
living room. You could hear them tramping their feet
to keep warm, and once he and the others spent half

[39]

an hour standing up in the little no man's land talking with the Germans. They traded newspapers and tobacco back and forth but a French officer saw the meeting and said, "You have a choice: get back down into the trench or be shot down by our own fire." So there was no more fraternizing.

Ex-Sergeant Major Polle was wounded when the Germans dug down and planted a mine. When it went off, he was knocked off his feet. The Germans came pouring into his trench and one of them fired a revolver at him as he lay on his back. The ball took him in the breast and went right through him. But he lived. Now in a light rain he looks for the precise spot in this formless forest which is marked on his daughter's Michelin map with the notation that the dugout of the Crown Prince was located here. During the visit three years ago M. Polle went with his daughter through a town where he remembered the name of a girl who had nursed him before he was evacuated back to a hospital. He even remembered what her house looked like and managed to find it again. The people in the house told him that she was long dead but that her sister still lived. She was not at home and they were going to send for her but he had no time to wait, he was only there for the day and wanted to find the

place he was wounded. So they went on but couldn't find the spot. Now he is back. He is sure he would know the place, for all the decades that have passed. It was not too long ago—no. He would know the place even though his eyes are too weak to read his daughter's map. And why does he want to find it? Why go back? He is silent. He is always that way, says his daughter. Never says much. But why does he come back?

"Well . . . I will not come back again. I don't have much time to live. It reminds me of my youth. I was near death here. Now I am near death again." He looks out into space. He raises his hands in a tiny gesture of perhaps two inches. He raises his eyebrows a little. "Why indeed? But I want to find the place."

The daughter says, "Here, Father?" and he says no, it is not the right place, not the exact place. He sits down on a folding chair taken from the trunk of the car and drinks a little wine and eats some cake. His daughter tells how the old people kept artillery shells on the mantelpieces of the houses of her childhood, polishing them so that they gleamed. Now not so many people do it—after all, it is not so interesting to keep polishing shells all the time. But still people plant flowers in them and still children find hitherto hidden

[43]

ones in the forests and take them to their little secret hiding places and try to open them up. Each year in the school—Mlle. Polle is a mathematics teacher in Lille—posters are put up with pictures of shells and grenades and warnings to the children that if they ever come across these things they are to tell an older person. But the children play with them nevertheless. (Everybody in France has long grown accustomed to two-paragraph stories in the newspapers saying the First World War has blown off the legs of another child.)

Monsieur Polle gets up and wanders through the old overgrown trenches and to the dugout of the Crown Prince. His daughter scrambles down to look at the pictures on the wall that some German drew of his sergeant or officer. But Monsieur is too old to go down the steps and he is growing tired. Gently his daughter suggests that they drive on to visit some of the graveyards. And so they go to the Forestière Cemetery a mile or two away. By the entrance is the Cemetery Register and she takes it out and reads off the names of men in his regiment. "Did you know this one, Father? This one?" But he does not recognize any of the names. So they drive on until they reach the tiny hamlet of Le Claon. He tells her to drive up a dirt road toward a little ridge. He was in the house there, he says, when the company was taken out of the line. They stop in front of the house and an old woman comes out. Heavy, wearing an old smock, she keeps one hand in the front pocket and rustles some papers there. The ex-sergeant major asks her if she was here during the war. She says she was. The daughter says, "My father was in the 82nd. He was in this house." The old woman begins to smile. Her hand shakes the papers in her pocket. She knows the 82nd, and all the others. She recites the numbers of all the regiments whose men were here. This house on her property was the hospital, and when boys died there they were buried under this apple tree. At the end of the war there were fifteen graves—or maybe it was sixteen. They are all gone now, removed to a big cemetery. Perhaps Monsieur remembers her farm as being grander then. Then all three houses were occupied, but now she is all alone and that is why things are not so neat. It was different before.

He asks her if the cooks didn't use to work here and she says that is true, they did. They had big fires going up on the ridge and at night men would carry food up to the line. They used to give her food to do their washing, and so she was never hungry in the war.

[45]

LOOS RIDGE, FRANCE. Dead horses and smashed wagons
lie by the roadside under a cloudy sky of late September of 1915.

Peter G. Masefield

LOOS RIDGE, FRANCE. The angle of the road is the same, and the distant town upon the horizon lives on, but now a British Army cemetery is by the roadside.

Imperial War Museum

MONS, BELGIUM. German troops parade through the Grand Place of the town remembered as the burial ground of the old professional Army of Great Britain which met the enemy in 1914's waning months. Its training and discipline were such that ordered rifle fire was thought by the Germans to be machine gun fire—so many of their ranks fell not to rise again. The Kaiser called it England's "contemptible little Army"; the few that lived through 1914-18 have ever called themselves the Old Contemptibles.

MONS, BELGIUM. The Grand Place in the summer of
1964 is jammed with automobiles; where the ornate bandstand
stood a tour-bus is now parked. Near where the German troops
rode is parked———a Volkswagon.

AMIENS, FRANCE. Summer, 1916. A column of Australian artillery passes through a street of the base-town of the British Empire's effort along the Western Front. Half a million men will fall on the fields lying just east of the road out of Amiens. Do the Aussies think about this? Do they notice the blocked-up windows of the two houses to the left of the picture? Who can say?

Peter G. Masefield

AMIENS, FRANCE. In 1964, there are trucks where once there were horses and private autos where once there were ambulances. The windows are still blocked up.

They were a lot of fun. They used to come into the houses and sing and dance and play jokes on her. They used to drink a lot of wine too. She laughs and he laughs with her in his quiet way. Does he remember when the people were forbidden to sell more wine to the boys because they drank so much? They spent all their money on the wine; it was expensive but it was better than the army *pinard*. Indeed he remembers, and it was good wine, too. And does he remember how the boys said, Well, if you don't let us buy wine, we won't go back to the line? Yes, he remembers that also. She laughs; he laughs. She ends her laughter and says, "Poor boys. The war lasted so long." The old man gets into his daughter's car and the old woman comes to the car window and says, "Thank you for coming." His daughter reaches out and touches the old woman.

La Ville-aux-
Bois-les-Pontavert:

Nine Hundred and Seventy-Three

THERE ARE several stories about how the Chemin des Dames—The Ladies' Way—got its name. One version has it that the road was constructed for the riding pleasure of two daughters of a French king. Another is that the women of nearby towns made it their favorite place for a Sunday promenade. It is some fifteen miles long and runs east-west in the center of the triangle of Reims-Laon-Soissons. Along the Chemin des Dames in the spring of 1917, General Robert Nivelle finished the destruction of France that was begun at Verdun. Promoted to commander in chief because of minor local successes at Verdun, Nivelle flung his army up the steep slopes leading to the road and into the very teeth of the enormously powerful German fortifications there. In a few quick days he threw away France's last great battle. Oceans of blood poured forth into the cabbage fields, and when he was finished France's Army was in rebellion. He had placed his men, at terrible cost, in a position militarily wrong and difficult to defend. It would have been far better to have withdrawn to the ridge lying south, but the name Chemin des Dames held the French on the road. They had spent too much to give it up.

The emphasis of the war shifted north and west to where the British were. The Chemin des Dames became known as a quiet sector, and after a time British troops were sent there to rest up after their battles. But in 1918, in Ludendorff's last great offensive, the Germans suddenly came pouring south, scattering the weak French and the few British and heading toward Paris.

In their rush the Germans rolled over the road which is just east of the Chemin des Dames. A section of that road, now N 44, was held by a few British troops, and most of the British along that road that day are still there. At the entrance to the cemetery is a large stone upon which is written THEIR NAME LIVETH

FOREVERMORE. The same kind of stone with the same
words is in every British Western Front cemetery save
for the very tiny ones. It is called the Stone of Remembrance. In every cemetery, regardless of size,
there is a stone cross—the Cross of Sacrifice. In this
cemetery, as in all the others, there is a book kept in a
metal container built into a little sheltered place by
the entrance; the one here explains that this cemetery
was created after the Armistice by collecting bodies
from the immediate area. Five hundred and forty iden-
tified soldiers and two airmen from the United King-
dom are buried in La Ville-aux-Bois-Les-Pontavert
Cemetery, and four hundred and thirteen men who are
Unknown. There are stones with the names of four
men Known or Believed to be buried in the cemetery
as Unknown, and eighteen stones commemorating men
buried elsewhere as Unknowns. In the book are recorded the names of all the Known dead. The cemetery is enclosed by a hedge and in part by a low rubble
wall. It is planted with poplars, birches, and thorns. "It
stands above the road, with wide views over the battlefields." The book was published by the Imperial War
Graves Commission (now the Commonwealth War
Graves Commission) in 1931.

There is another book; the Visitors' Book. Ever since

this cemetery was set up, there has been a Visitors'
Book in which one is requested to sign his name and
add any comment he likes. Every few years a book is
filled up with several hundred names and comments,
and is taken away and put in the Commonwealth War
Graves Commission files. And a new one is substituted.
There are more than a thousand British cemeteries;
there are tens of thousands of filled-up books dating
from the nineteen twenties.

In the Visitors' Book of La Ville-aux-Bois-Les-
Pontavert Cemetery last summer, W. C. Balfour, who
served with the 2nd Middlesex in 1918, wrote, "Thanks
my pals are here." A Frenchman wrote, "Remem-
brances of a poilu of 1914-18." Also in French was:
"Respects of a little girl nine years old." A group of
Germans from Munich visited the cemetery together
and wrote, "Brave dead soldiers." "Brave soldiers."
"Rest in peace soldiers." Mostly the people were from
England; they wrote, "Very well kept. Thank you."
"Thank you." "Beautifully kept—thank you." Fred-
erick Ronald Ransome wrote, "I have been so moved
to visit my father's grave." His father is among the
Knowns: Second Lieutenant F. R. Ransome, 1st Bn.
Royal Dublin Fusiliers attached 2nd Bn. West York-
shire Regt. died of wounds 26 May 1918. Two people

with the same last name of an Oxford boy: "I shall always remember." "I shall always remember." In a quavering handwriting: "On behalf of your brother Bert and family may you rest in peace, dear Ned. From your old friend Jim, still going at near 71." From a London woman: "*A little corner of a foreign field that is forever England.*"

Down the road perhaps the distance of a city block is a memorial erected to the Second Battalion of the Devonshire Regiment, which, the lettering on the stone says, repulsed successive attacks on this spot, thus permitting the defenses in the south to be reorganized and reinforced. "Without hope of assistance they . . . fought to the last with an unhesitating obedience to orders. Thus the whole battalion, Colonel, twenty-eight officers and five hundred and fifty-six noncommissioned officers and men responded with one accord and offered their lives in ungrudging sacrifice to the sacred cause of the Allies." The battalion was awarded the Croix de Guerre with Palm. By the monument is a little roadside inn and across the road a winding lane lined with white-painted shell casings from the big guns. All about are flat empty fields and dripping skies; here and there are concrete floors once enclosed with walls punctured with holes for the machine guns. In spots a bit of wall is still standing. There is a blockhouse used as a garage for the inn; on its side is a painted advertisement. The town built to replace that destroyed in May of 1918 lies a few minutes walk to the south. Perhaps it has a score of houses. Everything is very quiet—the shell craters, fields, low skies, the monument, the inn, and Tommy Atkins dead nine hundred and seventy three times.

Belleau Wood:

We Are Proud to Bear the Title

MOST OF THE survivors of this war now in U.S. Veterans Administration hospitals suffer from one of two ailments. One group is composed of those who were gassed and have been out in civilian life during the intervals when the coughing and gasping abate somewhat. (Now, when they are no longer young, the good intervals grow shorter and shorter, and so the wards paradoxically are growing more crowded as the war recedes into the past.) The other group is made up of men who went as boys to France in 1917–18 and through the quiet sectors up to the front. At the front (and sometimes even before it was reached) something happened to this group. One by one those slated to spend young manhood and middle and old age in hospitals manifested the first signs of illness. They began to talk too much. Or they fell silent. Whiz-bangs came over or machine guns rattled, and the men were medically beyond reach—"shell shock." They were taken back to the United States and today in the VA hospitals they watch television or play volleyball and work in the gardens. Relatives come now and then, and sometimes people who want to do something for them put on musical shows or take them in buses for a picnic. The broken men once boys rush for the hot dogs and anxiously ask, "Buddy, will there be enough?"

Once they formed up with the others who went on to life and the postwar world and who would wait expectantly for the American Legion conventions so they could use their electric canes on girls who were infants at the time of the Armistice. Those who would never drop paper bags filled with water from hotel rooms marched with those who would; they wore choker collars and wide campaign hats with bright-colored cords; they sang, "Goodbye Broadway, hello France"; they sang, "There's a long, long trail a-winding into the land of my dreams." Many of them arrived, with the others who would live and be well, and

[62]

with those who would die, at the long fields south of the Bois de Belleau. In that wood were the Germans who had poured over where the La Ville-aux-Bois-Les-Pontavert Cemetery is now; in that wood were machine guns with cross-fields of fire, and mortars, and riflemen shooting from bunkers and behind rock emplacements. The doughboys and leathernecks—mostly the latter—came walking through the fields with their heads bent down against the steel flying at them, and made for the shattered trees. In the ruined towns of Lucy-le-Bocage and Bouresches they froze when the big shells thundered over like express trains rushing through an endless tunnel to land with explosions lighting up the landscape that looked so like the surface of the moon. Their ration parties lumbered up Gob Gully past broken trees from which dangled horribly wet legs trailing undone puttees to the ground. Rifle grenades came down and lifted the horses up and left them as great hulks of meat grinning in death with the lips drawn back in the last act of life: a scream very like that of a woman in agony.

The boys crossing the fields up to the woods were not the U.S. Marines and prewar soldiers of legend; there had been no drinking in tough bars for them, no street brawls under tropical moons. On the contrary,

[63]

they were for the greater part college boys enlisted from their campuses to make the world safe for democracy. They came to these insignificant towns and this little meaningless road hardly more than a paved country lane, and did their fighting and went to their graves at home or in the great cemetery beyond the wood, or to their madhouses, or to civilian life and, within a very few years, to a terrible feeling that it was all a bunch of foolishness, and then, with the decades, to white hair and pot-bellies and increased incomes and grandchildren and winters in Florida.

They came and went. Belleau Wood remained.

Today Belleau Wood is the property of the United States government, a gift of France. It has a new name given it after the fighting: Bois de la Brigade de Marine. During the twenties and thirties it was the place every American tourist visited. Parisian cab drivers had a fixed price to take ex-soldiers there. Then came another war and today the tourists go to Normandy. But Belleau Wood is still beautifully tended. There is not a stray leaf or twig anywhere. The trees planted to replace those murdered by the screaming shells stand in long orderly military-like rows. (The boys-become-grandfathers who fought through those other trees do not present nearly so military an appearance today in

the newspaper pictures taken as presidential candidates address them in overseas caps.)

You can stay for two hours in Belleau Wood, where once the Yanks held the way to Paris, and see no one. Perhaps in the cemetery one or two gardeners are working, but the woods themselves are empty. It is as if unseen workers appear when the sun goes down and pluck the weeds and cut the grass between the endless straight lines of trees. In a clearing are old guns, painted black against the elements, rearing their noiseless mouths to the sky. They stand there silent and dark, waiting—and no one comes. Can there ever have been here what is called a great and glorious moment in history? Under the stones in the great cemetery are there really splintered and gashed bones, are there really the young buddies of the fat and bald old men laying off the calories and watching the cholesterol? Is it all true what Grandfather says, that here in this disciplined quiet place Major John Hughes sent word to headquarters that "I have every man, except a few odd ones, in line now. We have not broken contact and have held"? Where was it—was it here by this silent black mortar?—that twenty-three-year-old Laurence Stallings, who would live to lose a leg and write *What Price Glory,* lay cowering but remembering that his

[67]

General told him he must "pick up a rifle and lead with steel"? Is it in this quiet path with these carefully heaped-up leaves that the dead men lay piled one on the other as a barricade, and the bayoneted ones gasped out their last and, finally, Major Maurice Shearer sent word: BELLEAU WOODS NOW U.S. MARINE CORPS ENTIRELY? Or was it all a dream of long ago, an episode invented by the history professors to fill a paragraph saying that the American action and demeanor were bracing to the faltering Allies, that the Americans showed substantial dash in their charges? Was it all in never-never land, far from the America of today with its superhighways and television? Did America really produce in these fat old men and mental cripples the wonderful soldiery of what began as the last gentlemens' war, the last gallant war, the last splurge of romanticism and legends and plumes? Did it all really happen?

The Somme: *Doolis Hay*

ROLLING PICARDY is all flat with nothing high, with neat stone houses and long haunting roads going up to the horizon between the tall swaying poplar trees under which the British marched. In Amiens, the base for the entire British effort along the Western Front, there remains one thing utterly unchanged from the time of the war (until 1939, The War). It is Godbert's Restaurant. In those days the rear-line officers always made for Godbert's when they had a few hours free, appreciating the tasteful, quiet paved yard where the staff cars could be left in safety, and the attractive entrance. Today the yard is still quiet and the entrance is the same as it was. There was, and is, a lobby and two rooms. At the desk where the cheerful little fat *patronne* sat, the *patronne's* daughter sits now. The food was excellent then, and still is—Michelin gives it a high rating. At the beginning of the war Godbert's was unknown to the great of this world, but since then, praised in all the clubs along Pall Mall, it has played host to many famous names. "The Prince of Wales was here," says the *patronne's* daughter in frightful English, "when he came to dedicate the memorial at Thiepval. And the King of England was here. He sat right there. And during the war and after, Doolis Hay was here many times." Doolis Hay? "Yes, he was here when I was a child and I saw him."

Out along the roads east from Amiens and Godbert's, where Doolis Hay ate, thin-metal canisters of unexploded mustard gas lie under the soil and corrupt the growth of trees whose roots burrow down and break through. It is impossible to plant a straight row of trees along the Somme. The gardeners of the Commonwealth War Graves Commission have long since given up hope of ever seeing a straight row. Too much stuff is down there. "Stuff" is the canisters and boots and shells used to fill up the holes made by other

shells. And the bodies of those who answered Lord Kitchener's call: Your Country Needs You. Along the Somme the best, finest, sweetest of England's youth perished. They were all volunteers. In their long lines they rose from their trenches on the first day of July, 1916, and strode forward dress-right-dress and died that way—in long, perfect ranks, bayonets fixed, each man just so, with leather polished and metal gleaming. British pluck. Some were picked up afterward. Some were buried by later shells and only now come to light. You can sometimes tell who they were by their rings and watches and identification disks. Their pens, in some cases, it is said, still write with the ink put there half a century ago. That first of July was the worst day in the history of British arms.

English people come past the Somme on holiday these days, heading back from their vacations on the Continent. Knowing vaguely that Uncle Will died somewhere around here, they halt their cars and go out and wander among the graves (A Soldier of the Great War. Worcestershire Regiment. Known unto God; A Sergeant of the Great War. Royal Irish Rifles. Known unto God) and look for Uncle Will's resting place. They don't find it, of course, and eventually they end up in the Commonwealth War Graves Com-

[73]

mission office in Albert, where they learn that in this tiny area of northern France there are not tens, but hundreds of thousands of graves. They have grown up knowing that all Mum's boy friends save Dad died along the Somme, and all Auntie's, but they have never stopped to think of just how many graves there must be.

The C.W.G.C. officials and gardeners try to help them, and proudly detail the fact that every man who died for Great Britain and the Empire has his name, beyond a shadow of a doubt, written somewhere on a memorial. Either he is under a stone with his name on it, or there is a stone that says he is Known to be Buried in this Cemetery, or one that says he is Believed to be. Or on one of the great arches across France and Belgium it is written that he is Missing. Through the twenties and thirties the mothers and fathers and older relatives of people like these came out to France seeking, if not Uncle Will, then Father, or My Son, or Brother. Imagine—the high wing-collars and dress-for-dinner vanished, and the open touring cars disappeared, Ramsey MacDonald did too, and Stanley Baldwin, Geneva and Locarno, all the catchwords of Europe-between-the-wars, and through all this, the cloche hats and rising hem lines, the people kept coming. During the Second War the untended roses ran riot, and the lists of the buried and the Visitors' Books disappeared, but now it is all as it was meant to be. Forty years and more have gone by since the Armistice, and the veterans have their "ticket," their pension, and they've got time free, what with the kids grown up and on their own, and so they come out from Canada and Aussieland and Blighty. They wander through the graves with their old war books and maps in their hands. They smile and nod at the gardeners trying to help the failing trees whose growth is being ruined by the debris of half a hundred years ago. Sometimes on the roads they pass cars with "D" for Deutschland above the license plates, and these people also are looking for cemeteries. Their cemeteries, severe and cold, are maintained by the French at the expense of the present German government. There are no flowers in them and very few individual graves. Most of Germany's dead are Unknown. Their symbol is the piece of sculpture done by Käthe Kollwitz, whose son died in this war. Her work shows the mothers and fathers of Germany with heads bowed and eyes on the ground where their sons lie beneath the words: GERMANY MUST LIVE THOUGH WE MUST DIE.

Along the road up from Amiens to Albert, past

[75]

where the vast artillery parks and railheads were, the Golden Virgin of Albert stands high above the horizon, glittering, gleaming. Once that Virgin sagged over the shell-ripped streets from atop the church the British called the Cathedral, and the soldiers said that when she fell, England would lose the war. (A French engineer crept up and fastened the statue with thick steel wire. No sense taking chances.) The Britishers go through little Albert, where once there were thousands of gun limbers, ammunition lorries, artillery emplacements, forward transport parks—all the immense end product of a mighty world empire carried to the tiny cutting edge of the gigantic sword—and pass over roads where the hundreds of thousands marched and the great guns rolled and the poor silly cavalry horses galloped, on to where Peel Trench was, and Centre Way, and Dead Mule Corner. Out past the town you can see at plowing time just where the trenches were, for though they are filled in now, the contrasting whitish earth flung up from deep down by the shovels digging breastworks has spread and, in these fifty years, fattened out, so that a trench five feet across is now a thick line of twenty or thirty, winding across the levelled surface.

Many of the visitors at the cemeteries carry artificial

flowers made by the British Legion Poppy Factory and
meant to be placed in front of Known graves. Upon
the bases of the gravestones under the name and the
date of death are words which close relatives were
allowed to designate right after the war. In Loving
Memory Of Our Dear Horace Aged 21. From Mother
and Father and Family. . . . God Be With You Dearest
Tom Until We Meet Again. From Mother and All. . . .
Rest In Peace Sweetest Husband and Loving Father.
Alice and The Girls.

Ever there is that immense Western Front silence
that speaks of what was lost in those years and which
haunts all who come here. On the slight rises you can
stand up as no soldier could have stood and see graveyards in every direction. But you hear nothing save
now and then a distant car or tractor. There is nothing
else. Delville Wood, where the South Africans met a
terrible fate, is an empty park now. Only a lone sheep,
belonging perhaps to an absent gardener, grazes there.
Flies light on its droppings as once the flies lit on the
dead men, revolting the live ones as nothing else did,
not the rats nor the stench nor the bloated corruption
of those who once were laughing boys singing that is
was a long way to Tipperary. And indeed they sang.
As in all the Hollywood musicals of the thirties, they

sang. For this was the Western Front of the Great War where the legions went forth in their millions with the bands playing before them. It was really that way—going to the slaughterhouse of their generation they made music. But under these white stones—God's Will Be Done. Loving Mum—there are torn, broken skulls from which wonderful songs issued. Pack up your troubles in your old kit bag.

The Stump Road cemetery, one of the hundreds, very small, lies along a road so slim that only one vehicle can pass. An Englishman wrote in the Visitors' Book last summer: " *'I consider the machine gun to be a greatly over-rated weapon.'* Douglas Haig, Field Marshal."

Ypres: *Kenney*

IN THE YEARS just after the war all of the Salient was mud. The roads had vanished and rotting horse carcasses lay everywhere, providing limitless food for the giant rats. Overturned gun carriages lay half in and half out of the stagnant pools of water in the shell craters. It was difficult to cut down the few remaining trees; saw blades broke when they bit into the bullets and pieces of metal in the trunks. Machine guns rusted in the collapsed tunnels and dugouts, and Chinese laborers, brought over for military construction work, lived, forgotten by the departed British, in the cellars of the ruined houses. In the midst of all this were the

[81]

peasants coming back to reclaim their land. Belgium in those days had a kind of prosperity, for there was work for all. Laborers blew up the thick bunkers with shell powder and used the concrete for new roads. Gangs of men made a living by flattening out fields made as rough as the surface of the ocean during a storm. They did not charge the farmers for their work; their profits came from selling the metal under the mud. That metal filled thousands of trains pulling out of Ypres for twenty years.

By the time of the Depression, the Salient was functioning as a farming area. But during the early thirties, Belgium had thousands of unemployed. And so they came back to the fields and dug down farther than the earlier workers had gone. They used the long bars made for cleaning machine guns, shoving them down four or five feet and then examining the tip. Yellow meant copper was underneath; rust equalled iron. Vast ammunition dumps were found, with thousands of live shells, and a great home industry grew up. Its workers were men who knocked the detonation tips off the shells and poured out the powder and sold the metal. (Sometimes the trick did not work; scores of men died one by one in accidents.) Some of the shells were too dangerous to disassemble, and for these there were

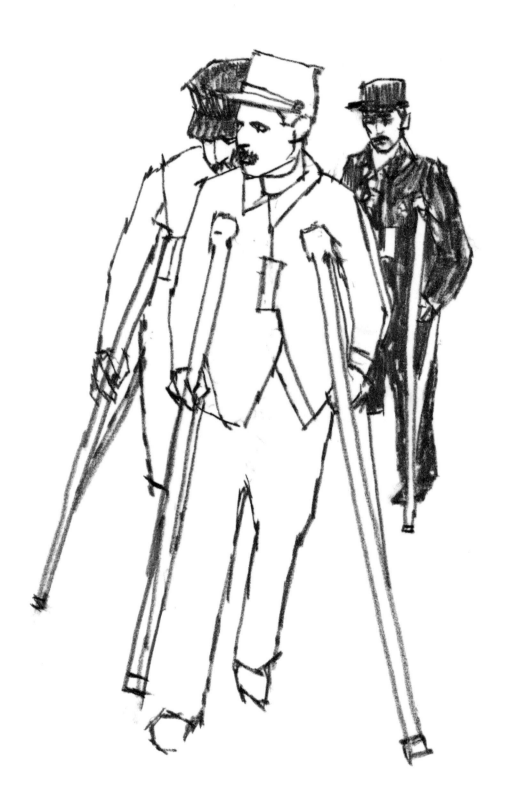

special fields where each day just before lunch and just before dinner red flags were flown to warn people away as Belgian Army experts detonated the shells and sent new blasts over the fields with the terrible names: Passchendaele, Wytschaete, Polygon Wood.

Throughout the twenties and thirties the armaments industry took most of the metal with which the Royal Artillery had all but broken the Bank of England. Then came the Second War and the business of collecting the old metal ended. But suddenly in 1950 the price of scrap in Europe doubled overnight: the Korean war meant cannons would be firing. Suez drove the price up also in 1956, but then it sagged and it is not high now. Still, however, men on the dole head out to the fields in the slow winter months. During rainy periods the metal seems to rise to the surface, cleansed of its clinging soil and shining dully. Traditionally in Belgium the proceeds from its sale goes for drinking money.

There is something else the Belgians find: men. In the winter of 1964, seven bodies turned up during the construction of foundations for a new foundry. Four bodies were found in February and three in March. The group of four were sitting on their heels with pistols in their hands and grenades strapped on. The

uniforms were still identifiable—good British material. You could read just what was in their minds: they were about to go on a raid and were waiting crouched in their trench. A shell came over and killed them by concussion and covered them with earth. Then there would have been other shells tossing up more earth and hiding the place where they were. So the four sat for fifty years holding their pistols and waiting for the foundry to be built so that they might come to light and be taken to a British cemetery in the Salient. Their hard rubber-like identification tags lasted, although the cords holding them around their necks were gone. There were no letters in the pockets, so the Graves Commission people did not have the problem of deciding what to do with them. (Years ago the rule was set up that letters addressed to family would be sent; those to girl friends would be destroyed.)

Ypres has always been the focal point for the British coming over to the Continent to tour the battlefields. During the period between the wars pilgrimages were arranged at cut-rate prices, and people bringing their sandwiches with them came over on the boat trains. They spent the day and went back that same night. Of course the motor coaches touring the more than 150

[86]

cemeteries could not stop at each one, so it was a common thing to see poorly dressed English people stopping citizens of Ypres on the street and pushing forward a few shillings to exact a promise that the Belgian would take a camera and go to a stipulated cemetery and take a picture of a certain grave and send the picture on. The well-to-do came oftener in private cars and sought the exact place where their sons died. They went down streets whose names they had obtained from the comrades of the dead, and knocked on doors saying that they understood their boy died in the cellar of the third house from the left at the end of the street. Now there seemed to be no house at all—and could the people help? Someone might be able to point to a heap of rubble and offer the information that this was where the house had been. The visitors would take pictures. One aged Englishman came each year to see a tiny wood. He said he derived comfort from being at the place where his only son died. He would sit for hours by himself; towards the end two men came with him in his big car and carried him out in a wheelchair and took a long walk while he sat.

Beginning with the summer of 1964, commemorating the fiftieth anniversary of the war's outbreak,

Ypres received a record number of visitors. For men who served in the Salient the city offered a handsome certificate with the ex-soldier's name on it. The city also held a little reception for those coming in organized groups. There were hundreds of such receptions. The men were taken to a large room in the city hall where an official handed out the certificates and made a short speech saying that Ypres paid tribute to all the dead of whichever side. "And now we will have a little drink and a smoke." Waiters moved forward with sherry and cigars. Then the men went to their waiting buses for the ride to the monuments and cemeteries. Some wore blue British Legion outfits of old regimental uniforms complete to clanking spurs and swords and silver braid down the sides of tapering breeches. In the silence of the great graveyards and memorial temples they moved, medals jingling, to seek the graves of friends, and then adjourned to little roadside taverns where they were expected and welcomed. (For haven't they kept those taverns going for fifty years?) Inside they got slightly potted, and their voices rose, and they took out their old paybooks and pictures of their companies and showed them around. There was always a refrain repeated endlessly as they pointed to the pictures of their pals: "He's dead . . . he's dead . . . he's dead."

[88]

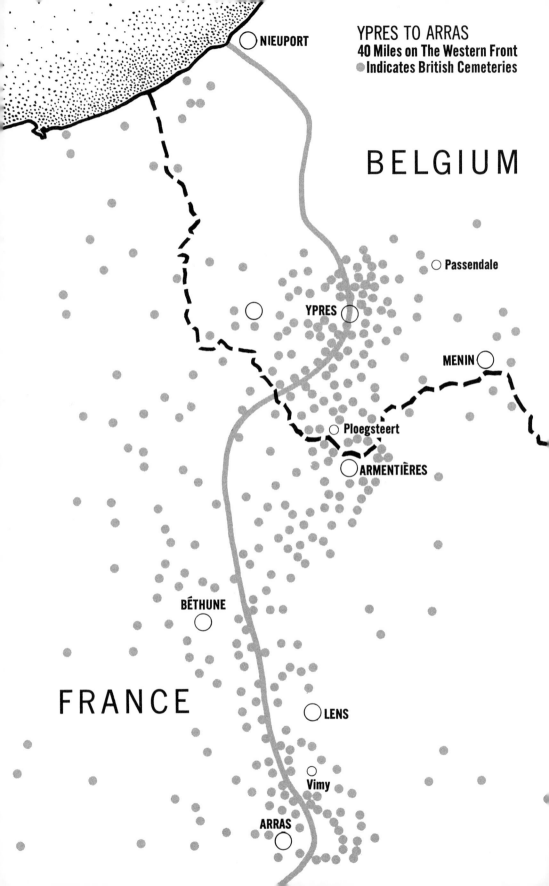

YPRES TO ARRAS
40 Miles on The Western Front
● Indicates British Cemeteries

BELGIUM

○ NIEUPORT

○ Passendale

○ YPRES ○

○ MENIN ○

○ Ploegsteert

○ ARMENTIÈRES

BÉTHUNE ○

FRANCE

○ LENS

○ Vimy

ARRAS ○

At the end of the long day and the many taverns, the singing in the buses rushing along the Salient's roads grew somewhat raucous, and men got out harmonicas and danced in the aisles. Some shouted in their Tommy French at passing women, and grew maudlin: "I live in England but my heart is out here." Others cursed the bloody Germans, or the wife of my bloody Colonel, "I was his batman, and she said she'd take care of me if I took care of him, and I did till he got his, but she went away to the South of France and I never heard from her again. . . ."

One man who came back to Ypres was quieter than most of the others. He was A. J. Arpal, who wore in his lapel the insignia of the Old Contemptibles Association, and who had seen it through from the very beginning. He had never been back since the war, but now with his grandchildren in school and his wife dead, he joined a tour which went all over the British zone, transportation, hotels, and meals provided for a week, at a price of only eighteen quid. Arpal was a cavalryman. His sergeant was Barnett, who rode a big chestnut and was a commanding type of man, inspirational. One day in a billet behind the lines, someone went mad and ran at Barnett with a sword. It was a sharp-pointed weapon with no cutting edge. They got

ZILLEBEKE ROAD, NEAR YPRES, BELGIUM. Armored cars go up the line past men of the Northumberland Hussars. A watching officer stands by a motorcycle.

Peter G. Masefield

ZILLEBEKE ROAD, NEAR YPRES, BELGIUM. On
the exact spot where the officer stood by the motorcycle, Dr. A.
Caenepeel of Ypres, an authority on the First World War,
stands with a young man and a motorbike. The house in the
background, rebuilt after 1914-18, bears scars of later conflict:
that which took place on this corner in 1940 when the German
Army attacked the British Army retreating in the direction
of Dunkirk.

FURNES, BELGIUM. Albert, King of the Belgians, stands
at the salute side by side with George the Fifth of Great Britain.
Behind them is the young Prince of Wales, later King Edward
and later still Duke of Windsor. The troops marching by are
Belgian.

Peter G. Masefield

FURNES, BELGIUM. The be-sworded and be-spurred
Royalties are gone, and so the troops, and so the flags; and a
young woman walks where stood the captains and the kings.

Imperial War Museum

THE MENIN ROAD, BELGIUM. Perhaps the most famous and most terrible crossroads of the entire Western Front: Hell Fire Corner. The Imperial War Museum's description: "The most hazardous spot of all . . . It was asking for trouble to pass it even at a gallop, and to attempt to do so at a walk was the equivalent of committing suicide. Thanks largely to the Ypres-Roulers railway, here crossing the road, the Germans knew the range to a yard."

Peter G. Masefield

THE MENIN ROAD, BELGIUM. The railroad still goes by; everything else is different. To know that their autos glide over where the hundreds of thousands marched to their deaths still brings a chill to those few who know that their way crosses what once was Hell Fire Corner.

YPRES, BELGIUM. British cavalry troopers ride through the Ypres-that-was. It is 1914 and soon Ypres will be a mass of unrecognizable ruins.

Peter G. Masefield

YPRES, BELGIUM. Ypres appears the same as it did in the days before the German artillery leveled the town. But in fact the medieval-like buildings are all post-1918, the living exponents of Belgium's desire that all be as once it was. Outside the town, nothing is as it was, however. For while Ypres was rebuilt in the old style, the outlying fields hold something irrevocable made by the war: more than 150 British Army cemeteries.

it away from the man. Other cavalry troops had sabres, but Arpal's had only this type. You practiced with it by jumping your horse over barriers and sticking balloons. Coming over on the transports with the first contingents of the British Expeditionary Force in 1914, the horses were like babies, sick and afraid to be left alone. They put their heads down on your shoulder when you led them down the gangways. Oh, the poor horses. Thank God they didn't use them in the Second War, because it was awful what they went through in the First.

For Arpal the symbol of that war has always been Kenney. Years and decades have passed since Kenney died, but Arpal has never forgotten him. Kenney was a laughing boy, twenty-two or three, and always wore his cap to one side. A happy kid. Arpal has thought of him a lot in these forty years while he has turned old and grey and quiet and a grandfather and Kenney has remained young in his lost grave in Belgium. Kenney represented the spirit they had in those days. Arpal was right there when this kid died. They were moving up in file early in the war and there was a volley of shots from beside the road. Kenney was knocked out of his saddle and Arpal thought to himself, Thank God he wasn't dragged by his horse. Arpal and the others

leaped into a ditch and opened fire. By next morning
the Germans were gone and Kenney was still lying in
the road. Arpal saw at once that it wouldn't have mat-
tered a damn if his horse had dragged him or not, for
he must have been dead before he hit the ground.
When they opened his coat to get his letters and
things, they saw that sewn into his collar where it but-
toned next to his throat there was a Union Jack. They
buried him but his grave soon disappeared in shellfire.
It was for Kenney's name that Arpal looked when he
came back to Ypres and saw the giant memorial where
the names of the Missing are inscribed in stone. Arpal
wandered through the tens of thousands of names and
saw all the ranks of all the familiar British regiments,
and those of the strange ones like the 9th Bhopal Infantry with its ranks of Suabdar, Jemadar, Havildar,
Sepoy. Finally he found Kenney's name, and all the
noise and traffic faded away. He had found Kenney.
That was at the Menin Gate.

Ypres: *The Menin Gate*

THE ROAD GOES eastward through the dreary little red-brick Belgian towns so like the industrial slums of England, and finally ends at the French border. At the road's beginning in Ypres is the Gate. They dedicated it in 1927. On the outside facing the road is inscribed:

TO THE ARMIES OF THE BRITISH EMPIRE WHO STOOD HERE FROM 1914 TO 1918. Inside: HERE ARE RECORDED THE NAMES OF OFFICERS AND MEN WHO FELL IN THE YPRES SALIENT BUT TO WHOM THE FORTUNES OF WAR DENIED THE KNOWN AND HONOURED BURIAL GIVEN TO THEIR COMRADES IN DEATH.

Kipling wrote the words. Underneath them are the
names of the Missing.

The featured speaker on July 24, 1927, was Field
Marshal Lord Plumer. Bandy-legged, with a puffy
face, not looking like a soldier, he stood with the King
of the Belgians before the giant audience come from
England. The reporters that day wrote that most of the
people were aged women, shabbily dressed. The South-
ern Railways ran special free trains to the coast for
them—first-class carriages only. The women bore
rambler roses, snap-dragons, lilies from their English
gardens. They sat in the hot sun facing the Gate with
their backs to the Menin Road leading out to the Salient, and six pipers of the Scots Guards standing on the
shell-shattered medieval ramparts by the Gate played
"The Flowers of the Fields." Buglers of the Somerset
Light Infantry sounded The Last Post, and to the reporters it seemed as if in the throbbing silence when
the calls faded away there must come some sound,
some sign, from the Salient up the road. Lord Plumer
cried, "They are not Missing; they are here," and the
Mums in their funny hats and long black stockings put
their hands over their faces.

After that, every night at eight in the winter and
nine in the summer, Belgian buglers sounded The Last

Post. In 1940 the Germans came down the Menin Road and took Ypres. For four years the buglers were silenced. But fifteen minutes after the last German was rounded up in 1944 the long slow notes of The Last Post quivered out from under the Gate. On some of the nights since then, particularly when the weather is bad, there is no one to hear the buglers except the policeman who halts traffic. At other times there will be a score or even a hundred people. Delegations come out from England, elderly men marching out of step and carrying old regimental flags. Age has shrunken most of them and made them puny, and for all that they are combat veterans of the Great War they look somewhat foolish as they line up in ragged files. Cars and trucks rattle under the Gate as they stand waiting for the police to halt the traffic. When this is done the flag-bearers go out and stand in the road. In the silence the sound of shuffling feet mixes with the dull rumble of idling motors. Someone shouts, "Attention!" and the skinny old men square-bash to something approaching the posture they were able to attain when all here, the living and the Missing, were young. Belgians—sometimes soldiers, sometimes members of the Ypres Fire Department—come marching out into the street to face the flags. There are often as many as

[104]

four buglers. They raise silver bugles given by the British Legion. Some of the old men salute in the British palms-out way. Others take off their hats. The beautiful trilling brings to mind hazy pictures of Indian garrisons and Sandhurst and Salisbury Plain; all the calls are sounded: Reveille, Mess Call, Defaulters' Call, Lights Out——The Last Post. When the final note dies the Belgians lower the bugles smartly, stand for a moment, and then wheel to the right and march to the curb. The traffic is already rolling under the Gate as the old men start to furl their flags. Some of them move back to look at the names on the walls yet again— Arpal for one last moment lets his eye rest on Kenney —and then the buses pull up to the curb.

About the Author ⌖

The Western Front of the First World War was less than 400 miles in length. But author Gene Smith logged more than 2,000 miles by automobile while exploring its front lines in the summer of 1964 in order to write this book.

Gene Smith's long time interest in the First World War was strengthened by the research done for his best-selling biography about the last years of Woodrow Wilson, *When the Cheering Stopped*, published in 1964.

Mr. Smith is a graduate of the University of Wisconsin and has served in the United States Army. He makes his home in New York City.